I0465257

CAREER AS A

SUPERMARKET MANAGER

TODAY'S SUPERMARKETS ARE A FAR CRY from the corner grocery stores that once dotted the American landscape from coast to coast. Supermarkets have evolved into stores that sell everything from frozen foods, fresh meats, fish, dairy products, vegetables, and fruits to packaged goods, pharmaceuticals, potted plants, flowers, balloons, prepared foods, baked goods, greeting cards and magazines, plus essential household supplies like glue, batteries, duct tape, automotive supplies such as motor oil, and even some basic appliances, including heaters, generators, propane tanks, and photographic equipment.

This radical change from simply selling food to filling store aisles with almost anything a customer might need has created a wide range of retail management jobs in the supermarket industry. Each new department added to a supermarket requires a manager to run it. That translates into executive jobs, as the supermarket industry keeps expanding to make its stores indispensable, one-stop locations for consumers to find anything and everything they are looking for.

New supermarkets are opening up throughout the United States all the time, especially in rural areas, as the population grows in those regions. While many parts of the US economy have gone digital, various aspects of the supermarket business just cannot be automated or are simply more efficient when there is a human being in charge. That includes having a manager on site who decides when and how to restock shelves, when to add cashiers to keep the checkout lines moving, and where to put free-standing displays. Individual managers also determine when particular items, especially perishables and prepared foods, should be marked down, and when to have staff circulating on the floor to respond to customers' questions and concerns.

The supermarket industry is very competitive. It is based on people returning to the store and having a positive experience every time they go there. Customer satisfaction is vital to the success of any supermarket, and department and store managers have to make sure customers are happy with how the store is run.

Even though most supermarkets today are part of large chains, each store is run differently. Some stores have more staff, are better stocked, are cleaner and brighter, and are more customer-friendly than others. Each store reflects the management style and philosophy of the management team, which should have a good understanding of their customers.

For instance, if a supermarket serves a largely Hispanic community, it has to carry a product line that appeals to its ethnic clientele, above and beyond the standard offerings. If it doesn't, another supermarket will open up that does cater to that community and will win over that customer base. It comes down to knowing what your customers like and need.

Supermarkets that are part of a national or regional chain have to answer to a corporate office. That creates another level of management in the industry and more jobs at higher salaries in the corporate headquarters. For example, every chain uses district managers from its corporate office to oversee the operation of its stores in a particular region. Other management jobs at the corporate level include marketing managers, who help promote stores and products in the stores, and category managers, who are in charge of store departments, such as dairy and meat, on a chain-wide basis.

Supermarket management is a fast-paced field because the industry is always following new trends in retail. That makes a job in supermarket management both demanding and exciting

---

WHAT YOU CAN DO NOW

SUPERMARKETS ARE EVERYWHERE, SO if this is the career you are interested in, you can easily observe the field firsthand. Go to several stores and see how they are set up. What makes each one different? Is the atmosphere friendlier at one store than another? Is the staff more helpful and responsive to shoppers? Is one store easier to navigate than another? Do the fruits, vegetables, meat, and fish look fresher and have greater customer appeal at a certain store? Keep in mind that you are a customer. Why would you shop at one supermarket rather than another? What attracted you and why? Make note of the pluses and minuses.

Working at a supermarket may appear to be easy, but nothing could be further from the truth. There are many moving parts to the whole operation and if there is a breakdown anywhere along the line, it could result in a loss of business.

Observe the inner workings of the store. Perhaps you can even spend some time with department managers and see how they do their jobs. Ask plenty of questions. Managers have usually been working at their jobs, and in the supermarket business, for a long time. They are generally eager to share what they have learned with others, especially students, who want to get into the field. In the supermarket industry, a great deal goes on behind the scenes to make the store operation run smoothly from the customer's point of view. That is what you have to master to be successful in the supermarket industry. By spending some time with the supermarket management team, you will get some valuable insight into how it is done.

HISTORY OF THE CAREER

WE RARELY THINK ABOUT THE ORIGINS of the supermarket. We just go there and shop, surrounded by all the conveniences of modern life. Yet how people got everything they needed to feed a family before the advent of the supermarket is certainly food for thought. Shopping centuries ago was quite a task. Before supermarkets as we know them began springing up in the 1930s, people had to go from store to store, buying meat at the butcher shop, bread at the bakery, fruits and vegetables at the greengrocer or produce market, seafood from a fishmonger, and packaged food at the grocery or the general store.

In cities, people generally walked to these mom-and-pop stores and carried their bundles home, because transportation was limited in pre-supermarket days. In the more rural areas, stores were a horse or wagon ride away, and this might take a day or so. Shopping was a burdensome chore. In addition, shoppers had little variety to choose from. Most of the stores were small – less than 1,000 square feet – and each only sold several hundred products.

Stories abound about how supermarkets came to be. There is plenty of credit to go around, but retailing took a giant step forward when A&P arrived on the American business scene. The company started out as a small tea business, under the name of Gilman & Company in 1861, and then became the Great American Tea Company in 1863. With the name change, the company opened five stores in New York City. It also used advertising to develop a substantial mail-order business.

The completion of the transcontinental railroad in 1869 prompted great enthusiasm throughout the nation. The founders of the Great American Tea Company, George Gilman and George Huntington Hartford, decided to play off the opening of the railroad and the euphoria surrounding it by renaming their company the Great Atlantic & Pacific Tea Company. Along with the renaming, the company introduced its own brand of prepackaged tea. Packaged coffee was also sold at A&P stores.

Fate helped the business expand. After the Great Chicago Fire in October 1871, the Great Atlantic & Pacific Tea Company sent their products to the Windy City to help out in the crisis. Within days, the company had opened a store in Chicago. It was A&P's first retail outlet outside of New York City.

By 1875, the company had stores in 16 cities, from Boston to St. Louis. Just three years later, it had 70 stores and brought in revenues of $1 million annually. Each store was run by a manager and staffed by clerks.

When Hartford's sons joined the company in the mid-1880s, they convinced their father to expand the product line and brand their own products. Over the next 10 years, the company added a number of products, including condensed milk, spices, and butter, and gradually became the first national grocery chain. By the turn of the 20th century, A&P had 198 stores throughout the country. In 1912, A&P introduced the economy store, which sold a full line of grocery products, and some fresh produce. These stores offered low prices on a cash-and-carry basis. That meant the stores did not extend any credit to shoppers, as some of the mom-and-pop grocery stores did.

A&P did everything to cut costs, which included finding inexpensive real estate and operating with as few employees as possible. A&P's low prices prompted outrage from traditional small groceries that struggled to compete.

An innovation from another supermarket founder changed the face of the whole business. In 1916, Clarence Saunders opened the first Piggly Wiggly in Memphis, Tennessee. Bewildered customers entered this new grocery store, where they were given baskets and allowed to select their own products from store shelves. Before this, even at A&P, store clerks had to get products for the customers. Piggly Wiggly had introduced self-service, something we take for granted today.

One of the technological innovations that propelled the growth of the modern supermarket was the automobile. The 1920s saw a tremendous surge in automobile ownership, and that meant people could not only drive to a grocery that might not be in their own neighborhood, but they could put their packages in the car. That led to grocery stores being built on large pieces of land so they could include a free parking lot.

In 1929, Michael Cullen, who was general sales manager at a Kroger grocery store in Herrin, Illinois, wrote a letter to the president of Kroger Stores. Kroger Stores had been founded by Bernard H. Kroger in 1883 as a tea company. By 1902, the company had expanded its product line and there were 40 stores in the Kroger chain. The company was known as the Kroger Grocery and Baking Company. It still exists today.

In his letter, Cullen spelled out the specifics of what would become the modern supermarket. Cullen's proposal included having everything the customer sought under one roof in a giant-sized store. With 40 stores in the Kroger chain, he said the company would have enormous buying power and would be able to negotiate excellent prices with manufacturers and distributors for the products the company sold. Kroger executives did not think Cullen's proposal would ever work, though the company now operates that way.

Cullen decided to invest in his novel approach to the grocery business. He moved his family to Long Island, New York, purchased an abandoned warehouse, and opened a store, called "King Kullen, the Price Wrecker," in March 1930. Two years later, in the depths of the Great Depression, he had seven more thriving stores. Cullen is credited as the founder of the supermarket, so the date of the first supermarket opening is usually linked to him.

The supermarket operation needed one more thing, and inventor/businessman Sylvan Goldman came up with that in 1937, when he invented the shopping cart.

The supermarket business took off in the post-World War II 1950s, an economic boom time for America. Numerous stores opened up, especially in the suburbs, as Americans started to move out of congested urban areas in favor of backyards and wide-open spaces.

Today more than 37,000 supermarkets operate in the United States. The Food Marketing Institute estimates that Americans spend $620 billion annually at supermarkets, with the average store carrying roughly 44,000 products. The typical supermarket encompasses about 46,500 square feet.

WHERE YOU WILL WORK

SUPERMARKETS COME IN ALL SIZES – small, medium, large, and even supersized – and they all need managers to run them. While the amount of stock, the size of the staff, and the numbers of customers may vary, the goal of each store is the same – to give customers the best possible shopping experience.

Supermarkets are located in busy urban areas, crowded neighborhoods, suburban malls, and the wide-open spaces of rural America. You can work in a supermarket that is surrounded by other stores and busy offices, or one that is out in the middle of nowhere, serving customers in remote areas who may have to limit their trips to the supermarket to once every few weeks.

Supermarkets are located in all 50 states and around the world, for that matter. They are one of the most recognizable retail outlets across the globe. So a career in the supermarket industry can take you almost anywhere.

Independently owned supermarkets and giant chains alike are always on the lookout for talented people to help run their businesses. It is not uncommon for one chain or store to lure gifted employees away from its rivals.

Chain supermarkets often shift their store managers and assistant managers to different stores in a region. This is usually done to put proven leaders in charge of stores that lag behind others in the chain, in hopes of strengthening these locations so they can catch up to the rest.

Department managers in a supermarket may find themselves working in various environments. The manager of the meat department, for example, is constantly in and out of the freezer. The manager of the frozen food department is in the cold most of the time as well. While the heat is always on for the person in charge of baked goods, the aromas coming from the ovens in the bakery are often irresistible.

The busiest times for supermarkets are usually the morning and evening rush hours. Depending on the size of the supermarket, store managers may be surrounded by a bustling crowd during these busy times. That can make your workplace quite hectic. By contrast, those working the night shift do their jobs in relative quiet.

Supermarket managers also work in hypermarkets. Hypermarkets are big box retail outlets that combine supermarket offerings with department store merchandise, like appliances and clothing. The supermarket aspect of the enterprise is run by a manager who is a retail food professional. The atmosphere in a hypermarket is somewhat different from that in a supermarket because the operation is not solely focused on food.

Supermarket chain district managers spend very little time in an office, though they often have a desk in the corporate headquarters. This is a job that involves many hours on the road. District managers are busy going from store to store in their region, solving problems, and making sure each store is running smoothly and is profitable.

Supermarket chains usually have large warehouses run by a warehouse operations manager. These warehouses are located in industrial areas off the beaten path, but inside they are a hub of activity as they get products to the chain's various stores.

Supply chain managers for supermarkets, as well as managers in marketing, category, innovation, and other areas on the corporate level, work out of the company's headquarters. These managers will sometimes find themselves on the road as well, to get a firsthand look at how policies and procedures are working on the store level.

THE WORK YOU WILL DO

WHEN YOU WORK IN SUPERMARKET management, you never have just another day at the office. There is always a lot going on and you have to be at your best. To get it all done takes planning, knowing all the tasks at hand for that day, and being prepared to handle the unexpected.

The workday starts early for most department managers and store managers, usually between 5 a.m. and 6 a.m. Supermarkets today have extended hours, staying open 16 or more hours, or even around the clock. Naturally, you cannot be there all the time, so one of your most important jobs is choosing the right person to place in charge when you are not around.

Store Manager

Managers hire employees all the time. Part of your job is being a good judge of character and being able to put the right people in the right jobs. Spotting talent will make your job easier because you will be able to assign a job to a person you know can get it done quickly and properly. You need to designate someone – and, in some cases, more than one person – who will be in charge during your off hours. The measure of a good manager is that you have developed a system for running the store that works even when you are not there. The person who takes over for you understands your policies and procedures well enough to run the operation without a hitch in your absence.

Department Manager

The modern supermarket is made up of numerous departments, including bakery, produce, meat, dairy, delicatessen, and many more. Each department contributes to the store as a whole. So every unit has to be run efficiently and effectively. That is the function of department managers.

People who run departments have to know their departments inside and out. There is the department that the customers see and there is also a great deal of activity that goes on behind the scenes. As a department manager, you have to handle all the components well.

Ordering

Ordering is a big part of a department manager's job and a store manager's job. On the one hand, waste eats into a department's and a store's profit. On the other hand, if you disappoint customers enough times by not having what they are looking for, they will start shopping elsewhere and you will lose customers.

Ordering is a delicate balance and a learning process, but you have to make quick decisions. Packaged goods can sit on the shelf for a while, but you still do not want these products gathering dust. Everything has a "sell-by" date, and your goal is to keep products coming in, and then make sure they go out before that sell-by date. Department managers and store managers have to know what sells in their stores, and what moves out quickly.

Much more prone to spoilage are fresh foods, such as meat, deli products, fish, fruit and vegetables, plus baked goods and other prepared foods. These items have a shelf life measured in days.

Department managers have to know how long these

products can remain in the cases, when they have to be marked down for quick sale, when they need to be repurposed (such as making unsold roasted chicken into chicken salad), and when they have to be disposed of. They have to develop a master plan with the store manager for when foods will be out on the shelves and when they will be removed.

In stores that bake their own products and prepare their own foods, managers have to know how much to prepare. That means studying sales figures so you know which are peak hours and peak days. Baking and preparing foods in a supermarket have added a new dimension to the business because commercial kitchens are subject to board of health rules. Areas where foods are prepared, or displayed and consumed, come under much greater scrutiny from government health agencies than parts of the store where packaged goods are sold. Supermarkets always have to be kept clean, but with prepared foods, store management has to make sure the food bars are pristine and dirty plates, napkins, cups, and utensils are not littering the store outside the eating area. If there is a food court, the tables must be cleaned and the garbage cans emptied regularly.

In produce departments, managers are constantly rotating the fruit, taking spoiled fruits and vegetables off display and replacing them with fresh product. Managers have to determine what can stay out and what has to be trashed. Most fruits and vegetables must be put away at night so they do not spoil. A manager might be able to get a customer a particular item, but, generally speaking, fresh produce cannot stay out around the clock. A decision has to be made about when this produce is put away and when it is put back out.

Supermarkets with deli counters close the counter at some point, even if the store stays open 24 hours a day. Certain deli products might be packaged and put in a refrigerated bin for self-service sales when the deli is closed, but the rest of the merchandise has to be put back in the freezer or refrigerator for sale the next day. Refrigeration temperatures have to be set properly and the entire deli area has to be cleaned thoroughly.

Most products are delivered overnight and that is when restocking is done. The store manager needs to know what deliveries are expected and when. Timing is important because staff must be on hand to unload trucks and restock shelves. You cannot afford to pay people if there is no work to be done, so managers have to schedule properly. This requires ongoing communication with corporate offices and distribution centers.

Customer Service

Customer service is very important. Not all irate customers demand to see the manager, but most want to talk to somebody in authority. Properly training the people (usually those at the courtesy counter) who have contact with unhappy customers is extremely important. That training is the responsibility of the store manager who makes it clear to those being groomed for that position how disputes are to be handled.

Customer service is about helping customers and satisfying them, not determining who is right and who is wrong. Choosing people who understand their role as customer service representatives and can keep their cool at all times will make your job as store manager that much easier. Customers can always lodge a complaint somewhere, whether it is with corporate headquarters or a government consumer affairs office, but you want to know that your staff does everything within reason to resolve any dispute that might arise before it escalates.

Pricing and Displays

Managers have to make sure pricing throughout the store is done correctly. Old signs advertising weekly specials have to come down as soon as the sale is over and new signs for the next sale have to go up. There can be no lag time. Improper signage only confuses shoppers and leads to misunderstandings.

Shopping is visual, so store managers are in charge of deciding where displays should go, rotating displays on a regular basis, and finding different ways of making those displays fresh and eye-catching. A mustard, ketchup, and relish display, for example, might take center stage in the summer, set up around a barbecue grill. Fresh and canned pumpkin could anchor a fall display, with hot chocolate and marshmallows setting the mood for a winter presentation. Displays like these help get customers in the mood for their favorite seasonal foods and spur impulse shopping.

Security

Security is another area that store managers have to focus on. Managers are concerned about the personal safety of their shoppers as well as safeguarding merchandise. Managers have to make sure parking lots are well lit for night shoppers. They have to know how many security people they need inside and outside the store to guarantee the safety of customers.

The heaviest losses a supermarket sustains come as a result of shoplifting. Part of loss prevention can be addressed by security, but part of it has to be handled by alert store employees who inform the manager when something is awry. Store managers also have to be ready to take action if they find out that an employee is stealing merchandise.

Consumers spend money in supermarkets every day and that means store managers have the serious responsibility of handling all this revenue and getting it safely deposited in the bank. The day's receipts have to be recorded. Each register has to balance out properly. The store has to have enough cash on hand to provide customers with change. The records have to be done properly and the manager oversees this process.

Department and store managers need to know their customer base well. Some stores may serve a large ethnic clientele that other stores do not. Having foods that appeal to those groups brings another dimension to your store. For instance, if a store is located in a heavily Jewish community, such as New York City, there would be more kosher foods available at that store. Traditional Japanese foods are more commonly found in supermarkets in places with a large Japanese population, such as Seattle.

Supervising and evaluating employees are also part of the manager's job, as is resolving any employee disputes.

District Manager

Supermarket chains usually have district managers who supervise a number of stores in a particular region. District managers make sure all the stores they oversee are following corporate policies and procedures. They check to see that sale merchandise is available and priced as advertised, the stores are running smoothly, customers are satisfied, the stores are properly maintained, financial records are in order, and the ordering of merchandise is being done correctly. They also handle any problems that the management team at the store may have with corporate headquarters.

Most district managers do not announce when they are going to visit a particular store. They just drop in because they want to see the natural flow of the business without anyone making special preparations to "impress the boss."

Corporate Management

In corporate management it seems as though everybody in the chain is counting on you and, in reality, they are. You are making decisions that impact the entire chain and you are doing it in a rapidly changing economic climate. Today you see departments in supermarkets you never thought you would see there, like food courts and coffee and wine bars. Who comes up with these ideas? It is usually the **innovation manager**. The innovation manager, who works out of corporate headquarters, assesses customer needs and identifies shopping trends. Then the innovation manager develops a strategic plan for meeting these needs and implements new programs that will put the supermarket in the forefront of the latest trends and in a position to respond to future trends.

Sometimes this means adding a new department and cutting back on an old one, or adding a line of products like those geared for people who want organic foods or gluten-free products. At times it can be about making the store more responsive to community needs, such as providing childcare for shoppers or changing stations for babies. Whenever you see something new in a supermarket, the innovation manager came up with the idea and made it a reality.

One major growth area in supermarket management is **supply chain managers**. Many of the tasks done by supply chain managers used to be done by individual managers in the corporate headquarters. That led to repetition and overlap of duties. Now supply chain managers are involved in everything from planning, purchasing, and production, to transportation and distribution. This is a big job with a great deal of responsibility and a large staff of assistant managers to go with it. By carefully managing all the areas they oversee, supply chain managers can save companies substantial money by avoiding duplication of effort in ordering and distribution, negotiating better prices with wholesalers, and streamlining the entire chain's operation.

Merchandising managers develop techniques for promoting stores and products in the stores. They give store managers ideas about where to place slow-moving items to draw more attention to them, and make suggestions about how to promote certain departments in a store, like giving out free cake slices so people become familiar with the store's baked goods.

Merchandising managers also evaluate where items are placed in stores and determine if there could be better placement. They discuss merchandising plans with manufacturers to see if the makers of a particular product want to engage in a more proactive plan to market their product in the store.

Another area of management is **loss prevention**. Sometimes this management post is held by a person with a law enforcement background, but many times the position goes to someone who has managed a store and knows about the loss prevention problems store managers face. The job involves developing loss prevention strategies using the latest technology to cut down on shoplifting.

Warehouse managers usually run a supermarket's distribution center. They are in charge of making sure the right merchandise is shipped to the right store and every order gets out on time every day.

Management titles in the corporate headquarters vary from chain to chain. Overall, the job at corporate headquarters is to make sure store managers have everything they need to run an efficient operation on the retail level.

SUPERMARKET MANAGERS TELL ABOUT THEIR CAREERS

I Am a Produce Department Manager at a Large Supermarket

"I think the focus on healthy eating and eating fresh has really propelled the produce department into the spotlight.

When supermarkets first opened, the produce department was always in the rear of the store. In the mid-1970s, the industry changed the way it looked at produce and started moving produce departments to the front of the store. Now it's a focal point – the first thing customers see when they come into many supermarkets. There are some very important reasons for this and one of them is marketing.

Merchandising is visual, and what has more natural visuals to attract customers than produce? That, however, puts the pressure on produce departments to make attractive color spreads and displays. So the job now calls for some artistry. We want to draw customers over to the produce department with our displays of fresh produce and get them to look at all we have to offer. It may sound strange, but we want people to get excited about produce. It becomes very important that we put out the freshest produce, and that anything that spoils is removed quickly. We want people to be enticed by our fruits and vegetables.

I try to have a member of the produce department on the floor at all times so people can ask questions about produce they might not know anything about. I also like to introduce produce into our store that is not seen or found in any other store. I don't mind telling people what it is, where it comes from, how to eat it, and how to prepare it. To do that you have to be knowledgeable about the produce you are selling and aware of the trends. People don't realize it, but there are trends in produce. People will get excited about trying a particular fruit or vegetable, and you have to know what it is and where to get it.

I like to talk to the customers and hear what they like and, more important, what they want. Listening is an important part of this job. But I cannot be the only one listening on the job. I teach everyone in the produce department to listen and have an exchange with customers. I am not here the entire time the store is open, so I need my employees to help me out and tell me what customers are looking for.

Most produce department managers come in very early in the morning – around 5 a.m. or so. Produce is usually delivered either overnight or very early in the morning. I do inventory and place orders so I know I'll have what I need the next day. My store gets produce delivered six days a week. Since I come in so early, I usually leave about 2 or 3 p.m. There are times I let my assistant manager handle the morning chores so I get a chance to mingle with the evening crowd and see what produce is moving quickly and what is not.

Interestingly, I spent several years after high school working on a produce farm and got a good background in produce from that. Then I decided I wanted to work as a produce manager in a supermarket. I started as a clerk and literally had every job in the produce department until I became produce manager. I learned things all along the way, and not just about produce. You learn about merchandising, customer service, and many aspects of the retail business. People are very particular about their fruits and vegetables. They don't want to see bruises or nicks, so you handle everything with care or it could wind up as waste, and that's wasting food."

I Am the Manager of a Major Supermarket

"I want my employees to be excited about the job they are doing every day. I am. I want them to have positive energy on the job. We have a very important responsibility. We are helping people in their daily lives. We have two rush hours a day, and we need to get people in and out of the store with what they want. I don't want it to be shopping here that makes people late for work or ties people up when they are trying to get home. If I am, then when they need something at the supermarket they are going to say, 'I don't want to stop there before work – it's a hassle' or 'I don't want to go there after work – I never get out of there.' Then, I'm losing customers, the best customers, because they are people who need something.

So I have my employees ready for the big rush. We have products on the shelves. We are ready to show people where things are and we are ready to check people out. I always say to my employees, 'Pretend you are a customer and you are trying to get to work. Let's not be the one who causes them a problem today.'

Handling the rush is only part of the job. The supermarket manager has to make sure the store is running on all cylinders. We have a lot of departments and every one of them has to be at its best. That means we have to think ahead.

Do we have everything we need for tomorrow or the big weekend coming up? We can't run out of hot dogs for the Fourth of July or coleslaw or baked beans or watermelon. That takes planning. I meet with my department heads every morning. I check with them throughout the day. We are always watching what sells and what we need to order. We never want to be caught short.

If you come in and out of here with no problems and think nothing about the time you spent in here, other than you got everything you came for, we did our job. That means we have been working pretty hard behind the scenes, ordering products, stacking the shelves, putting sale items on display where you can see them, cutting the meat, putting out the fruit, and baking the bread. It goes on behind the scenes seven days a week, and if we do it right you hardly realize what a big job this whole operation is.

I'm not here to sit behind a desk, and neither is anyone else in this store. There is always something that needs your attention, whether it's cleaning the restrooms, getting the shopping carts out of the parking lot or making sure we have enough cashiers at the front end.

I like an employee who is walking past a register, sees an order piling up, and grabs a bag and starts bagging the order. That's spirit, that's teamwork, that's customer service. And you know something? I do that myself. It's simple and maybe a bit old-fashioned: We are people helping people – that's how I see it."

I Am a District Manager for a Large Supermarket Chain

"I have a district that is made up of a dozen stores in two states. Sometimes I cover more stores if someone is out on vacation or leaves the job and a new district manager has not yet taken over.

This is definitely not a desk job. I visit each store in my district at least twice a week – more if there is a particular issue that needs to be addressed, like making space for a food bar, expanding a department, or making decisions about renovating an entire store.

I worked my way up the corporate ladder, starting out as an assistant manager on an entry-level basis, and eventually managing a store in the chain before moving up to district manager. As part of my training, I spent a good deal of time in every department and I learned about everything that goes on in the store. I know and understand the problems store managers face every day, and I have experience in handling those issues.

I think the first thing a district manager has to understand is that while all the stores are part of the same chain, they are still individual stores. These stores serve different populations, in different areas, and have to meet different needs. As a chain, we have to meet all those various needs and provide each store with the support required to serve their special customer base.

Everything has to be taken into consideration, from the way we order products for each store to the hours the store is open. Are we serving the community by having self-service checkouts in a particular store or are we just causing a bigger backup at registers at that store with automation? Are we responding to customers' needs by having prepared food in a particular store or has the reception to the prepared food been lukewarm? That is, are we just wasting a lot of food? Everything is relative and we keep looking at what we are doing and reevaluating what is going on in our stores and the industry as a whole.

I am sort of a middleman. I speak for the stores on the one hand, and corporate headquarters on the other. I let corporate headquarters know what's going on at the store level and what managers and employees think about new policies and procedures. I let people on the store level know what is happening on the corporate level and why. I try to get both sides to understand each other's point of view and influence decisions so that both sides get what they want and need, to make this the best supermarket chain around.

There have been times when I have taken people from the corporate headquarters and brought them to stores to see why an idea they had just won't work in our retail outlets. I have convinced managers to give an idea that has come down from the corporate office a try before dismissing it out of hand. I like being able to work out a compromise that benefits both sides because in the long run it benefits our customers.

I've been a district manager for 10 years. This job never gets boring, and I am able to accomplish a great deal. I find that the work I am doing is appreciated on both the store level and in corporate headquarters. That's a good feeling to have in a job."

PERSONAL QUALIFICATIONS

BEING A MANAGER MEANS BEING A LEADER. You will call upon your leadership skills time and again if you choose a career in supermarket management. Leaders are strong and decisive. They have to instill confidence by making good decisions quickly and getting results. Leading by example is a store manager's credo. Managers dress appropriately, project enthusiasm, and are courteous to employees and customers alike.

Successful managers are able to motivate their employees. They give everyone who works for them a voice in the process of making the department, store, or corporation better, so each one has a stake in how things are done. That means challenging employees to excel in their jobs, to set lofty goals, to meet those goals, and to go on to achieve even greater things.

As a manager at either the store or corporate level, you will encourage your employees to offer suggestions about how to resolve issues they see on the job every day. You never dismiss an employee's idea, even if it has been tried before and has not worked. Instead, you discuss the suggestion with the employee to see if that worker has a different take on the proposal that will make it successful this time around. Welcoming new ideas, making revisions, and tweaking suggestions are among your key attributes.

As a supermarket manager, you take a personal interest in every employee. You get to know your employees' hobbies and children's names so you can mingle with the staff on a person-to-person basis at times, rather than just having a boss-to-employee relationship. That special interest makes employees want to go the extra mile for you. If they have a problem on the job they feel they can come to you and speak freely. The ability to inspire employees helps managers command respect from their staff. The talent to get the most out of every employee every day makes you a managing success.

Delegating responsibility is an ability shared by good managers. They do not fear letting someone else take charge and are quick to praise a job well done.

Communications skills are vital when you are in charge. You have to let employees know what is expected of them and what the goals of the store and the company are.

Listening skills complement your ability to communicate, and you are not just listening to employees. You also value the input of customers, whether they have come into your store for the first time or are regulars. Customers have to feel that store management cares about them and responds to their concerns.

Top-notch managers have an eye for detail and are well organized. Creativity is also part of the job description, since managers often design displays that feature products. These displays have to attract customers and enhance the decor of the overall store.

Being a proven multitasker comes in handy in this job, as does being a good teacher. Not only do managers train employees, they also mentor them. Many of the employees you hire will move on to become managers themselves and they will have learned the job from you.

ATTRACTIVE FEATURES

BEING IN MANAGEMENT GIVES YOU THE opportunity to be creative, to express ideas, and to learn and grow in your job. You have the power to make positive changes and help people. You can put your ideas into action and watch as they enhance the shopping experience in your store. You will take pride when problems are solved, schedules and procedures are running better, and your innovations are implemented.

Every day is different. You face diverse challenges and learn from each situation.

Those in management can move up quickly, either in the supermarket where they currently work or in a competing supermarket or hypermarket. In fact, your experience is valuable anywhere in retail sales, whether you decide to go to another supermarket chain or another type of retail outlet.

Managers are respected because they are given responsibility. People seek you out for your professional expertise, advice, and guidance. They trust your decisions and have confidence in the moves you make. Managers are recognized as part of the executive level for the store and the company as a whole. They are often consulted by company owners who seek their input on issues involving the future of the company.

Good supermarket managers enjoy the loyalty of their employees. People want to help you carry out your ideas and succeed in realizing your vision for your department or store.

Supermarket management is a hands-on job. You walk the aisles, greet the customers, work with and get to know the employees. You will not spend much time behind a desk.

Everyone likes an upbeat, happy workplace, and supermarket managers are the people who shape that work environment. You have the power to keep the store or office as stress-free as possible. You can establish a friendly and welcoming atmosphere for both customers and employees.

Managers are usually salaried employees, rather than hourly wage workers. Raises and bonuses are awarded to supermarket managers who achieve good results. In addition, these managers receive paid vacations and a benefits package. Managers also get discounts when they make purchases from their own store. Whether you are a supermarket department manager, a store manager, or you work in a management position in a supermarket chain's corporate headquarters, complaints come with the territory.

You will hear about problems far more often than you will receive compliments for the work you do.

UNATTRACTIVE ASPECTS

YOU GET COMPLAINTS FROM BOTH employees and customers. Some problems you can address and resolve, other complaints may be unwarranted, and some things may be beyond your control. Keeping everyone satisfied is how you retain customers and maintain a pleasant, upbeat work environment. Being a problem solver can be one of the most stressful parts of your job, but one of the most critical. People often think you have more power than you do and wonder why you cannot straighten out every situation. Getting people to understand that you are as frustrated about a problem as they are can be exasperating.

You will encounter people working for you who think they can do a better job or just want your job. Being second-guessed can be annoying. Your decisions are often based on information only those in management know about, including budget, inventory, and staffing constraints. Managers have to make tough choices. Sometimes, as a result, you will not be very popular with the people working for you. The old adage is true when it comes to management positions: It's lonely at the top. Good managers are not hesitant about making hard decisions. Even if you assign an employee to do a job and that person does the job badly, it is ultimately your fault. You were the one who thought that person could handle the assignment, but you made a bad call.

Overall, supermarket management jobs come with pressure. The smallest matters will come to your attention and you will have to handle them. Managers often put in longer hours than anyone else on the staff. If you cannot find anyone to work nights, weekends, or holidays, you will end up doing it yourself.

There is a high turnover rate among lower-level employees in supermarkets, like entry-level clerks and checkout people in stores. If you are a store manager, it will seem as though you are always training somebody new to fill a job at your store. Managers on the corporate level in supermarket chains constantly have to train entry-level administrative assistants to replace those who have moved on to higher-paying jobs, even in the same company. So training personnel can take up a great deal of your time.

EDUCATION AND TRAINING

SUPERMARKET MANAGEMENT REQUIRES a variety of skills. Those going into the field should have at least a high school diploma, though a college degree or certificate will help you climb the corporate ladder much faster. Many community colleges throughout the country offer certificates in retail management. Some even have programs that are specifically geared to the food industry. These programs generally take a full-time student only about one year to complete. Certificate programs are an excellent way for you to prepare for a career in supermarket management. When you complete the certificate program, you can enter the workforce, continue studying full time for an associate degree (usually requires one additional year) or bachelor's degree (usually requires four years total after high school), or take a job and study part time for your degree.

In the western part of the nation, the nonprofit Western

Association of Food Chains (WAFC) has partnered with a number of community colleges to provide students with a comprehensive retail management certificate program that takes about a year to complete for full-time students. There are more than 135 community colleges in 13 states in the western United States, including Alaska and Hawaii, that offer the WAFC-endorsed retail management certificate. Courses in the certificate program include Principles of Management, Financial Management and Budgeting, Business Communication Skills for Managers, Principles of Markets, and Human Resources Management.

Some of the community colleges offering the WAFC-backed certificate program are Bellevue College in Washington; Central Arizona College in Coolidge; Klamath Community College, Klamath Falls, Oregon; and City College of San Francisco and Fresno City College, both in California. A complete list of colleges participating in the WAFC retail management certificate program can be found at:

retailmanagementcertificate.com
/for-students/participating-colleges

Two colleges offer this retail management certificate program online to students nationwide. They are Cerritos College (California) and Umpqua Community College (Oregon).

The WAFC has also partnered with the University of Southern California (USC) Marshall School of Business in Los Angeles for several programs, including a 15-week course of study resulting in a certificate in food industry management. The program is usually offered during the spring semester on campus. Courses incorporate a variety of subjects, such as global competition, decision- making, strategic planning and analysis, and financial management, to give students wide-ranging insight into the retail food business. In addition, USC has an intensive four-day food industry executive program designed for those in high-ranking management positions. The course of study enhances the skills of people in executive positions by delving into topics that address the rapidly changing landscape of the retail food business on the local, regional, nationwide, and global levels.

There are numerous programs in community colleges and four-year schools for those who want to study retail management or food industry management. One of those schools, Suffolk County Community College on Long Island, New York, awards a two-year degree in retail business management to students who complete a program that features courses in Retail Management and Operations, Business Law, Retail Principles, and Computing for Business, among other subjects. The school also offers a certificate in retail business management, which takes less time to complete but is not as comprehensive as the two-year degree program.

The University of Wisconsin-Stout in Menomonie offers a bachelor's degree in retail merchandising and management. Purdue University in West Lafayette, Indiana is another college with a bachelor's degree program dedicated to retail management, and Purdue's has internships to go with it.

Saint Joseph's University in Philadelphia offers a bachelor's degree in food marketing. Many students with this degree have gone on to corporate management positions with supermarkets throughout the country. The school also has a master's and a post-master's program in food marketing.

Michigan State University in East Lansing has a well-established food industry management program for students who want to go into either the retail or the wholesale side of the food business. The program results in a bachelor's degree and has a large number of advanced management courses. Students who have studied food industry management at Illinois State University in Normal have also gone on to numerous jobs in the food business, including as corporate executives in the supermarket business. This program is offered as a sequence to students majoring in agriculture at the college.

Some colleges, like the University of Pittsburgh, the University of Memphis, and the University of Rhode Island in Kingston, offer majors in supply chain management, which is a growing field in retail, especially in the supermarket industry. Retail management, food retail management, and supply chain management are all areas of job growth, with more and more colleges starting to offer majors or minors in these specialties, primarily in their business schools.

No matter which course of study you pursue, most supermarkets – especially the chains – require new employees to attend extensive training programs the company has established. These help immerse you in the job and the corporate culture. Then on-the-job experience leads to promotions, but a good educational background before you apply for a job will get your résumé noticed, help you land the job you want, put you on a management track, and start you off with more money.

EARNINGS

THE FIRST THING TO REMEMBER about earning a paycheck in supermarket management is that these employees are paid a salary, rather than an hourly wage. Generally speaking, people who are on the management track from the start of their careers have some post-high school education and bypass the lowest entry-level jobs. Salaries are good and come with benefits like paid vacations, medical and dental insurance, and even retirement packages.

Assistant managers in stores usually earn between $30,000 and $40,000 annually. Salaries do increase incrementally as you get more on-the-job experience. Department managers in supermarkets earn from $55,000 to $70,000. Depending on the size of the store and the experience of the person in the job, store managers can earn anywhere from $75,000 to $125,000. The $125,000 plateau can be eclipsed by store managers in very high revenue stores, such as a chain's top-producing store.

District managers usually start out at about $80,000, even more if the corporate office is trying to lure the person away from a good-paying store manager's job elsewhere. It is not unusual for district managers to earn $150,000 at the peak of their careers.

When it comes to working in a supermarket's corporate office, salary depends on what level of management you start at and the size of the company. Some people bypass the store level and enter management at the corporate level. They may have earned a college degree or completed some internships that prepared them for corporate management positions. They start out as assistant managers on the corporate level, earning roughly $50,000 annually, but they are still learning on the job, gaining experience, and moving around a lot, as they try to find out where they can best use their talents.

When they settle in after getting to know the business, these people generally land jobs like innovation manager, supply chain manager, loss prevention manager, or merchandising manager. Some of these jobs are higher on the pay scale than others, and salary also depends on experience. An experienced supply chain manager can earn between $175,000 and $200,000 a year. A loss prevention manager will earn less than that, probably in the $150,000 range. In corporate management, paychecks are often based on results.

OPPORTUNITIES

THE SUPERMARKET INDUSTRY IS CONSTANTLY changing in response to new customer trends and preferences. In fact, supermarkets stand out today as one of the businesses that implement changes the fastest when it comes to addressing consumer demands. That opens up new management opportunities in the industry all the time. The latest growth area in supermarkets is prepared food. Prepared offerings have increased tenfold from the days when roasted chicken was the only item on the menu. Now a wide range of prepared foods can be taken home or consumed on site. Supermarkets with food courts and dining areas attract large lunch crowds. Takeout for dinner from supermarket food bars is more popular than ever, competing with fast food restaurants. Some supermarkets have even gone into catering. These expanded areas of the supermarket industry all require people to manage them and that translates into job growth. Jobs in supermarket management are expected to grow by seven percent over the next decade, according to industry analysts.

It was not that long ago that bakeries were a rare sight in supermarkets. Customers demanded more than the standard packaged breads that were customary in supermarkets for decades. They wanted fresh bread, muffins, and cakes. Stand-alone bakeries could not respond to that need with competitive prices, but supermarkets could. Not only did this addition of bakeries create jobs for bakers, but also managers, on the store, regional, and corporate level as well. The industry found that people coming in for freshly baked bread and pastries also bought some other items that they might not have otherwise made a special stop to buy. Bakeries in supermarkets became a boost to the entire industry. It was a development that few saw coming, but it added foot traffic in stores and jobs in the business.

Other opportunities are springing up as well, as specialty supermarkets offering ethnic foods or healthy eating open their doors throughout the nation. The trend toward healthy eating is the bailiwick of supermarkets that focus on providing their customers with only natural and organic foods. This is more than a passing fancy, as more people choose to eat natural and organic foods. Supermarkets that solely provide these foods are expanding throughout the country, opening up jobs for managers on all levels of the corporate ladder. The same is true of supermarkets in ethnic communities that provide foods far from the standard fare that is seen in general supermarkets.

In a busy nation, where people are trying to squeeze more into their day, supermarkets are responding by staying open later, some even 24/7. The efficient supermarket always has a manager on duty, making sure shoppers get the same quality service around the clock. It is what makes shoppers choose one store over another, and it creates jobs for energetic, dedicated managers committed to customer service.

GETTING STARTED

MANY COMPANIES SAY THEY PROMOTE from within, but in the supermarket industry that is usually the case. Getting an entry-level job leads to promotions, and if an employee shows promise, the climb up the corporate ladder does not take long to begin.

Most supermarkets hire entry-level management associates. That does not mean you won't bag groceries or stock shelves, because managers often pitch in during busy times to handle the rush. It is all part of the job and the learning experience in supermarket management.

One thing most supermarket chains seek in an employee is somebody who knows about and understands the food business and the specific supermarket chain, in particular. Corporate executives like new employees to get a feel for the business and the company by working in various departments in the store, seeing how things are done, and getting a grasp of the corporate philosophy.

There are many supermarkets and you can choose to work at any of them, so it is a good idea to do some homework before going out in the workforce. Most supermarkets have informative websites, where you can read about the company and see what kind of opportunities they offer, including the types of benefits that are available.

You can also visit different supermarkets and see which ones have the type of environment where you would enjoy working. You can tell a lot about a store just by walking down the aisles. What type of product selection does the supermarket offer? Is the store well-maintained? Are the product displays eye-catching? Do the employees seem to care about the customers? Does the supermarket have enough staff or does one employee have to run from department to department to help customers? Is the store in the vanguard of the latest innovations in the field, or does it seem to lag behind other supermarkets where you have shopped? Talk to employees and see how they feel about the store and the company.

These observations will give you insight as you plan your career path. Reading supermarket trade publications like *Supermarket News* and *Progressive Grocer* will give you valuable information about breaking news in the field with regard to employment. All supermarkets are not created equal, so take the time to do the research and find out which company suits you the best. Some people enjoy working for large corporations and seek the nationwide advancement opportunities those companies offer. Others would rather join a smaller, regional company, where they are more likely to stay close to home and work in an atmosphere where they are not lost in the corporate maze.

Another decision is where in management to work. Do you want to work on the store level or in the corporate office? Is there a specific department you would like to pursue? This is a wide-ranging field that calls on a variety of talents, all requiring knowledge of the food industry.

ASSOCIATIONS

■ **National Grocers Association**
http://www.nationalgrocers.org

■ **National Supermarket Association Global (NSA Global)**
http://www.nsaglobal.org

■ **Western Association of Food Chains (WAFC)**
http://www.wafc.com

■ **United Fresh Produce Association**
http://www.unitedfresh.org

■ **Produce Marketing Association (PMA)**
http://www.pma.com

■ **Northwest Grocery Association (NWGA)**
www.nwgrocery.org/home.html

■ International Dairy-Deli-Bakery Association (IDDBA)
https://www.iddba.org

■ National Co+op Grocers (NCG)
https://www.ncg.coop

■ Independent Grocers Alliance (IGA)
http://www.iga.com/about.aspx

WEBSITES

■ Food Marketing Institute (FMI)
http://www.fmi.org

■ Grocery Manufacturers Association (GMA)
http://www.gmaonline.org

■ Fresh Produce and Floral Council (FPFC)
http://www.fpfc.org

■ Food Industry Alliance of New York State (FIA)
http://www.fiany.com

■ The Institute of Grocery Distribution
http://www.igd.com

■ National Fisheries Institute (NFI)
https://www.aboutseafood.com

■ International Foodservice Distributors Association (IFDA)
https://www.ifdaonline.org

■ **American Association of Meat Processors (AAMP)**
http://www.aamp.com

■ **National Retail Federation (NRF)**
https://nrf.com

Copyright 2016 Institute For Career Research

Careers Internet Database Website

www.careers-internet.org

Careers Reports on Amazon

www.amazon.com/Institute-For-Career-Research
/e/B007DO4Y9E

For information please email service@careers-internet.org

www.ingramcontent.com/pod-product-compliance
Lightning Source LLC
Chambersburg PA
CBHW061233180526
45170CB00003B/1282